101 Positive Pictures
by Inspired Cartoons

Written and Illustrated
by Robert Valentine

Copyright © 2019 Robert Valentine

The moral right of the author has been asserted.

Apart from any fair dealing for the purposes of research or private study, or criticism or review, as permitted under the Copyright, Designs and Patents Act 1988, this publication may only be reproduced, stored or transmitted, in any form or by any means, with the prior permission in writing of the publishers, or in the case of reprographic reproduction in accordance with the terms of licences issued by the Copyright Licensing Agency. Enquiries concerning reproduction outside those terms should be sent to the publishers.

Matador
9 Priory Business Park,
Wistow Road, Kibworth Beauchamp,
Leicestershire. LE8 0RX
Tel: 0116 279 2299
Email: books@troubador.co.uk
Web: www.troubador.co.uk/matador
Twitter: @matadorbooks

ISBN 978 1838590 512

British Library Cataloguing in Publication Data.
A catalogue record for this book is available from the British Library.

Printed and bound by CPI Group (UK) Ltd, Croydon, CR0 4YY
Typeset in 22pt Brandon Grotesque by Troubador Publishing Ltd, Leicester, UK

Matador is an imprint of Troubador Publishing Ltd

For Dawn, Ruby, Lacy, and our star in heaven.

I know that if I get out of bed early to watch the sunrise,
it could inspire me to lead a better life.

I know that living in the past gets me nowhere.

I know it's good to have goals, but I must remember to not constantly live in the future.

I allow negativity to bounce off me;
I refuse to let it in.

I know people will laugh or judge me for being different, but I must be me.

I FOLLOW MY PURPOSE

I feel better when I am following my purpose. It took me a while to find my purpose, but it was worth searching for it.

I must learn to control my ego
because nobody is better than anyone else.

RELATE BUT NOT INTERFERE

I know it's good to relate to my past, but I need to make sure it does not interfere with my present.

I know it's better to admit I'm wrong
if I am wrong.

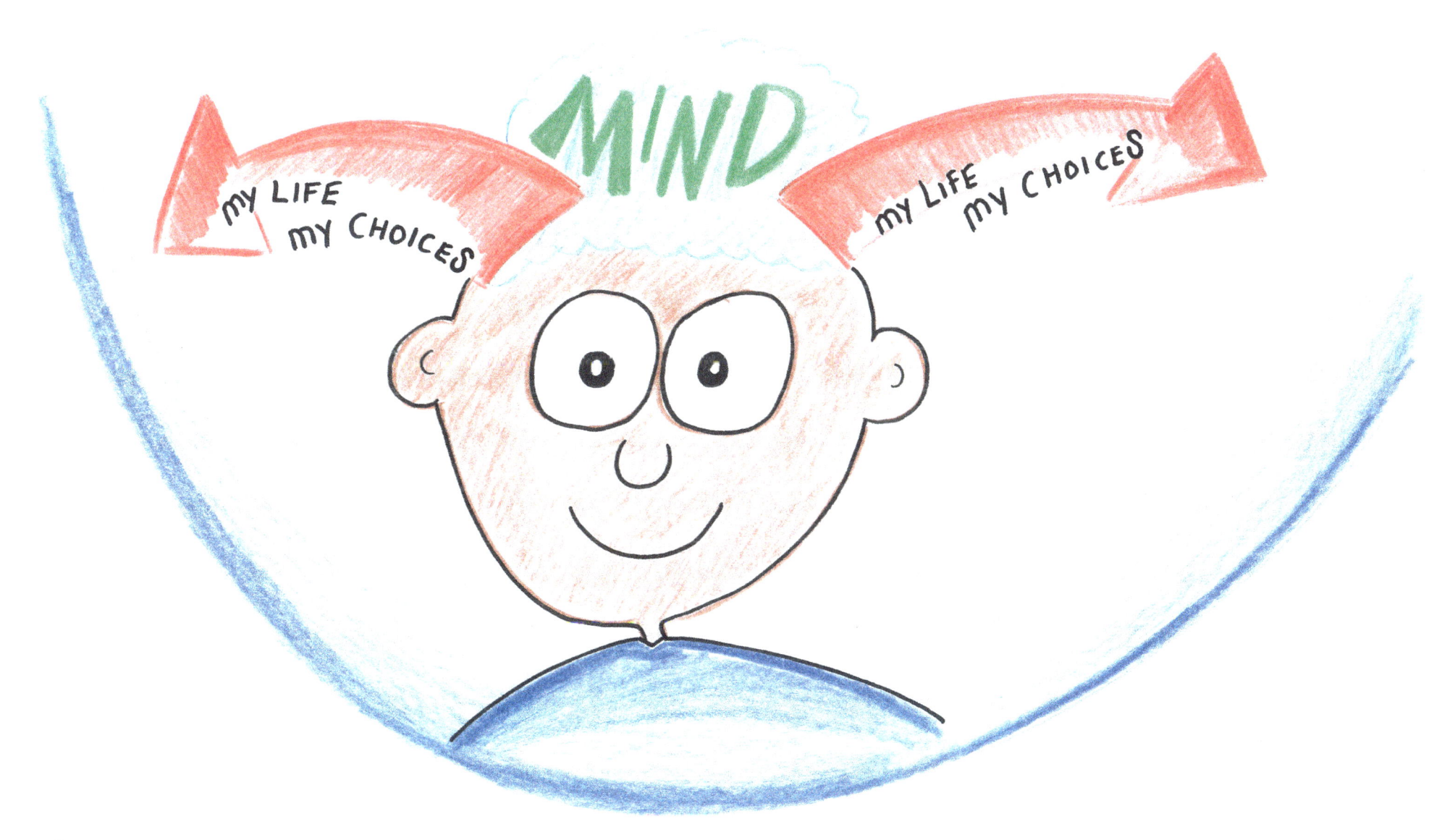

I know the greatest thing I own is my mind.

I must look after myself sometimes.

I understand that years of building trust can be broken in seconds.

I know we can all spread love
and kindness like butter.

I know that overthinking will destroy me.

I must understand there is no point in talking if I have nothing to say.

I know if I listen more, I will understand more.

I know that surrounding myself with positive people will help me become more positive.

Although it's difficult to understand,
time will help me accept emotional pain.

I know that when I give to others
it makes me feel good.

I know that helping others is the best thing I can do.

I know I must try to manage my time better
and not let it run away with me.

Bereavement
Pain
Shock
Guilt
Denial
Anger
Depression

Acceptance
Hope

LIFE ON

**Although it's difficult to understand,
life will go on. I must accept it.**

I must focus on my positive head voice
more than my negative head voice.

I know that negative people could eventually make me more negative. I must keep my internal smile.

I can focus on my breathing
when I need to relax.

I must remember I cannot be anywhere else than where I am now.

I must remember everyone is different and everyone can do different things.

I know the world is round, so why do we try
to put everything into boxes?

READ A BOOK

LISTEN TO SOME MUSIC

GO TO THE CINEMA

ZZZZZ OR JUST HAVE A NAP

I know it's OK for me to save my energy and make time for me occasionally.

We are all the same, but everyone is unique,
and therefore it's OK to like myself.

I accept I am the actor in my own 'Life Play'.
I play the main character in my life, and therefore I am in control of myself and my actions.

I accept I am the filmmaker of my own 'Life Film'.
I am directing my own life, and therefore I can edit out all
the bad stuff and focus on all the good stuff!

I don't want to waste my twenty-four hours
a day just hanging around.

I am quick to point the finger at others and blame them, although often the problem is me and I can't accept it.

I must follow my heart, even if others disagree or simply don't like my choices.

I know to receive love and kindness I must project love and kindness myself.

I know the longer I carry hate around with me, the heavier it becomes.

I KNOW IT WILL BE OK WHEN I'M THERE... BUT I CAN'T **STOP** WORRYING ABOUT IT.

IT'S OK IN THE PRESENT

I always worry about the future. I must realise that worrying is a waste of time because things are never that bad when you're there!

"Come and watch this horror film! It's brilliant"

"Er... great"

I understand we are all different and like different things.

I don't want to be famous. I want to be significant, and I think everybody should feel significant.

I will try to understand if someone is rude to me; they could be having a bad day and I don't know their circumstances.

ANYWAY YOU CAN, THERE IS ALWAYS A WAY TO HELP OTHERS HELP OTHERS

I believe we should all be kind and fair, treating others with respect.

RELIGION GENDER SEXUALITY DISABILITY SKIN COLOUR

APPEARANCE AGE WEIGHT AGE WEIGHT SEXUAL ORIENTATION

PHYSICAL RACE DISABILITY GENDER

PLACE OF ORIGIN

"A PERSON'S PAST CHOICES....."

I will not judge people on their...

I need to know where I am flying my plane before I take off because if I don't know where I am going, I will never get there.

I must realise most people are too busy thinking about their own lives to be bothered with gossiping about mine.

I really must stay in control of my emotions.

I must stay hydrated with water
to stay happy and focused.

I understand life is about seasons...
so are humans.

If my life was a car: I must make sure to put the right thought processes into my car.

I know we are all different and unique,
so why do we learn the same things the same way?

99% IN PLAN "A" — *I WILL FAIL, AND CREATE PLAN "B"* — *ONLY IF I BELIEVE*

I must believe in my plan 'A' 100%, otherwise my mind will automatically create a plan 'B' and simply accept I failed plan 'A'.

I know I cannot please everyone.
If I was a cake, there wouldn't be enough slices to go round.

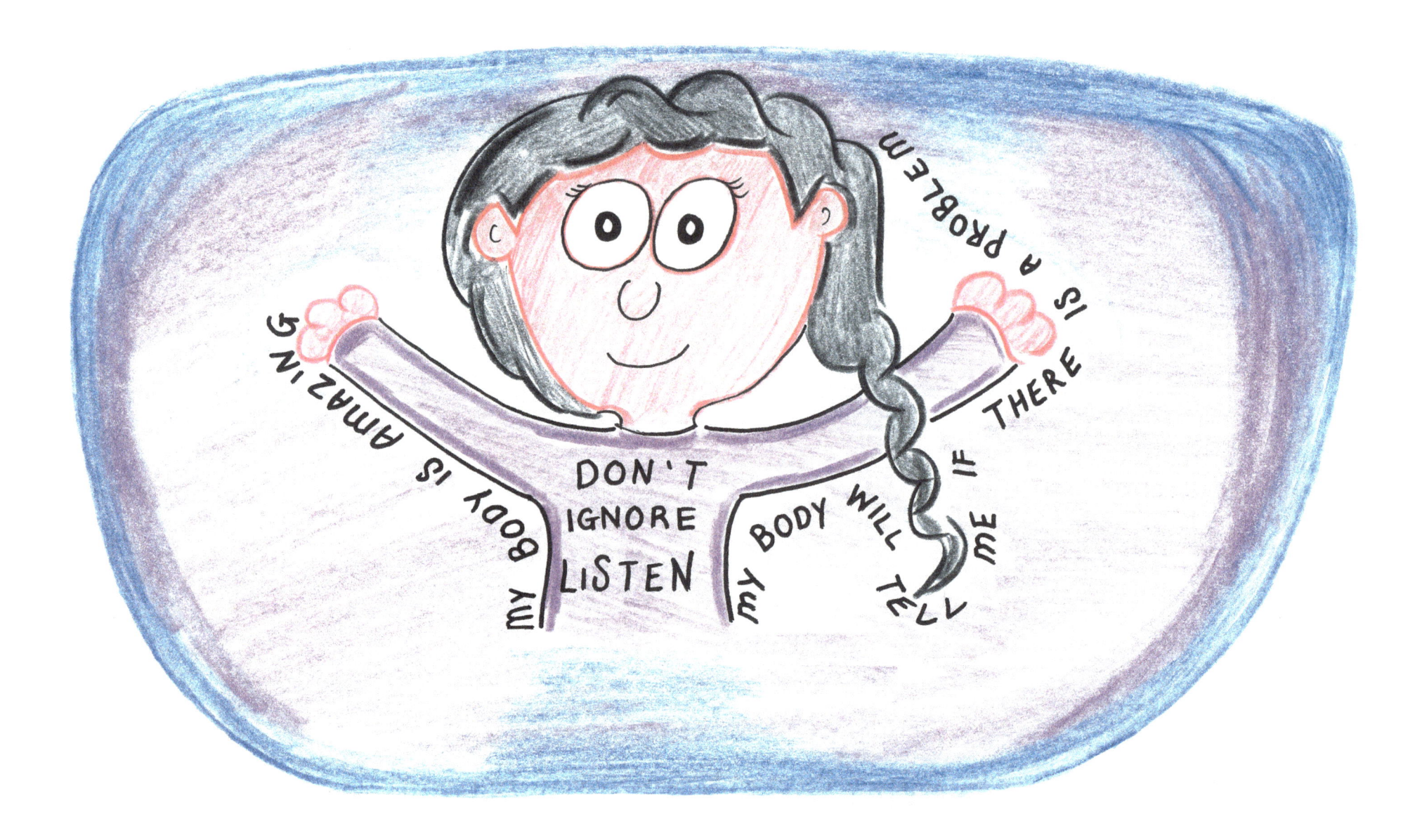

I shall not ignore my body if it tries to tell me something.

I like to exercise to release endorphins, which naturally make me feel good.

I wish I knew why so many of us
just go through the motions.

I know I should enjoy
most things in moderation.

I know I talk to myself, and that could be considered madness.
However, I think ignoring yourself is totally bonkers!

I am 100% sure these babies were not born racist.

Racism is learnt behaviour.

I need to remember the world owes me nothing.

Sometimes life isn't fair. Life goes on; I just need to get on with it regardless.

THINGS I TAKE FOR GRANTED

PEOPLE WHO CARE FOR ME   FOOD   CLEAN CLOTHES   FRESH WATER   WARMTH

There is normally someone worse off than me, although often I forget it.

I can focus on happy thoughts
when I need to de-stress.

I must accept that eventually my lies will come round to bite me when I least expect it.

I know that I just need to take the first step towards my goal and then continue one step at a time.

As a baby I was determined to walk.
As a young adult I've developed an 'I can't' attitude.
I just need find the 'I can' attitude I used to have.

I must remember forgiveness does not mean I'm weak.
It means I'm a better person.

I know there is one solar system and one human race.
However, there are billions of egos making everything difficult.
Lose your ego.

I plant positivity seeds to allow positive outcomes to grow (PS = PO)!

Of course I try and try again.
However, I am wise and know when to quit
if something isn't working for me.

I must remember there are two sides to every argument and story!

I know it's good to make shopping lists, but why do so many of us forget to make an affirmations list? Affirmations help your mind build positive thoughts!

THE SAME

I WANT THINGS TO STAY

CHANGE

WILL

HAPPEN

I must remember that nothing stays the same and change is always going to happen.

I will not be scared to show my feelings and emotions.
It is not a weakness, but a strength.

I know I could master anything if I practice it for twenty minutes a day!

I could be a master at my chosen activity in five years if I practice everyday.

I am the computer programmer of my own mind.
I will only program positive thoughts.

I know that kindness is free.

I know I cannot buy happiness;
I simply choose to be happy instead.

Poo or ice cream?

It all depends how you look at life.

It's how we look at the glass of life. It's either fantastic or rubbish.
It's the same glass though, so clearly it's a choice.

MIND

HEART

GUT

Deep down I know what to do for every situation because I feel it in my body.

STARS

WAVES

SUNRISE

SUNSET

I take time to enjoy the free stuff.

I know the key of creativity
will open many doors.

I must make sure I don't gossip behind people's backs.

I know words can hurt too.

I know we all experience things in life, but I must remember it's how you ride the wave that matters.

PEOPLE WILL JUDGE YOU THROUGHOUT LIFE

I am here to be me.

I must be the master of my own mind.

Sometimes I need to take a break from work, and I need to remember that's OK.

I need to realise real friends are real friends.
Not people I need to impress.

I need to remember
I cannot force anyone to like me.

It's my mind and I will decide what to let in.

I must remember not to sink in the swamp of negativity.

I need to remember to stay calm
even when I'm in the middle of chaos.

"NEGATIVE THOUGHT" — I WISH I WAS HAPPY

"POSITIVE" THOUGHT — I WILL BE HAPPY

POSITIVE ACTION — SMILE — BE HAPPY

I know I am what I think I am and if I follow it with 'action', then I get results.

SUCCESS AND POSITIVE OUTCOMES

I can visualise my success; I can then turn the visualisation into positive actions.

I am everything I choose to be.
It's all inside me already.

It's black and white. My life is going so quick.
I must remember to enjoy my life while I have it.

I always go down the same path.
However, I am going to change my path to get different results.

When I have made the decision to do something,
I always give 100%.

I know watching the sunset can help me appreciate
my life and be grateful for all that I am.